THE 30-DAY LYRIC
WRITING CHALLENGE

THE 30-DAY LYRIC WRITING CHALLENGE

ED BELL

Bell, Ed
Book : The 30-Day Lyric Writing Challenge

Library of Congress Control Number: 2019905950

ISBN 978-0-9981302-3-1 (Paperback edition)

Published June 2019
New York City

CONTENTS

ABOUT THE SONG FOUNDRY

At The Song Foundry it's our mission to share great songwriting ideas with the world. At thesongfoundry.com we publish articles about songwriting, host free videos on various songwriting topics, and offer Skype songwriting coaching worldwide.

Connect with us online to find out more:

thesongfoundry.com

youtube.com/TheSongFoundry

facebook.com/TheSongFoundry

twitter.com/TheSongFoundry

INTRODUCTION: HOW THIS WORKS

Hello – and welcome to *The 30-Day Lyric Writing Challenge*, a series of short but powerful challenges to get you writing lyrics smarter and faster.

The only way to become a better songwriter is to get plenty of practice, so that's what these thirty challenges are going to help you do.

Each challenge is designed to take exactly 10 minutes, so plus the two or three minutes you'll need to understand what each challenge is and why it's important, setting aside 15 minutes each day for 30 days is all you need to do to complete the full set.

When you do the challenges is up to you – but it's a good idea to pick the same time every day to help make it become a habit. (Pro tip: first thing in the morning is a *great* time – before work, family and any other life distractions get in the way.)

All you have to do to complete the challenge is commit to those thirty daily slots, spend a moment to make sure you understand each challenge, then start the countdown and do nothing else until the time is up.

If you've read my book *The Art of Songwriting* you'll know I'm not a huge fan of songwriting drills or exercises because I think the best way to improve your songwriting skills – by far – is to try things out and go where your curiosity leads. So in creating these challenges

I've made sure to keep them far away from any kind of abstract drills and exercises: they're genuine, real-life things songwriters do to turn a blank page or screen into a finished lyric.

And because they're challenges more than exercises, you can bring whatever level of skill you have already – without feeling like you're out of your depth or they're way too easy – and the challenges will still push you to level up on each particular skill.

You're going to practice coming up with new song ideas. You're going to practice coming up with useful rhymes. You're going to practice rewriting lines to simplify them. And you're going to practice coming up with details and specifics that can make a lyric shine.

As you work through the challenges, I'm also going to tell you a bit about *why* the challenges matter – not only what you're doing but why (and how) it's going to help you as a lyricist. I'll do that to try and explain why these challenges are more than just exercises and to help give you the drive and perspective to give the challenges your best shot.

With each challenge I'll also give you a target to aim for – something like, 'come up with at least six perfect rhymes for each of these words.' They're all based on what seems like a challenging but achievable goal for most songwriters. Of course, you might not be most songwriters, and that's fine: if you don't quite hit the target some days, that's fine, and if you reach the target well before 10 minutes is up, that's also fine – just keep going until the time's up.

Either way, quality is much more important than quantity with these challenges – and most important of all is sticking out the 10 minutes, without fail, for 30 days in a row. As I said, the only way to improve your songwriting skills – or any creative skills, for what it's worth – is by putting in the time and putting in the practice. So if you want to see results, it's up to you to stick it out.

I designed the challenges to take 10 minutes each day partly so you can focus on one specific skill in each challenge, but also so they'd fit into any daily schedule. If you're super keen and have time, you could do two or three challenges each day and get through them in less than a month. I obviously recommend sticking to the 30-day plan, but as long as you find thirty regular slots to get through the challenges, it's all good.

One last thing – you'll need a pen or pencil and a blank pad of paper for the challenges. And I definitely recommend you save what you create, in case you want to use any of those ideas in a real song later – you never know what might come in useful.

So there we are. That's pretty much everything you need to know before you dive in.

So let's do it.

[DAY 1]
THE PERFECT
RHYME CHALLENGE

[DAY 1]

THE PERFECT RHYME CHALLENGE

For your first challenge, let's start with something straightforward: a perfect rhyme search. As you probably know, rhyme is a really common and effective way of giving a lyric structure and making it easier to remember.

Sure, in real life you might use the Internet or a rhyming dictionary to help you find rhymes, but you also want to be quick at coming up with them on your own.

Quick reminder: perfect rhymes are exact matches like 'cat' and 'hat', not 'cat' and 'hurt'. They can also be more than one syllable: like 'cravat' and 'acrobat'. Watch out for identities – like 'fine' and 'define', that just repeat '-fine' – and also any words you have to mis-stress to force a rhyme – like 'LOOK-ing' and 'Bei-JING'.

> **Why it matters:** Training your brain to churn out rhyming words – especially rhyming words that are connected in meaning – on demand is an essential songwriting skill.

DAY 1 CHALLENGE

 10 mins

Find <u>at least six perfect rhymes</u> for each of these words:

      [1] hair

      [2] set

      [3] show

      [4] shine

      [5] long

You can try cycling through the alphabet – 'at', 'bat', 'cat', 'dat' … – but also try free associating: resting your mind against the word and seeing what other words it sparks.

For bonus points, try to find rhymes that are connected in meaning – e.g. 'late' and 'wait', both about time – and/or rhymes that are more unusual or unexpected somehow.

And like I said in the introduction, if finding thirty rhymes in ten minutes is a walk in the park for you, that's great. Just keep going. See how many more you can find before the time's up.

[DAY 2]
THE COLOR
CHALLENGE

[DAY 2]

THE COLOR CHALLENGE

Today's challenge is about reaching for the perfect word. Writing music in songwriting is much more about the overall vibe or feel, but lyric writing is a different challenge because your specific word choices can have subtly different effects on the lyric overall.

In general, lyrics work best when they're simple, but a great lyric usually steers clear of anything too obvious or clichéd. Sometimes, reaching for a word that's not hyper-unusual but equally not everyday is a way of turning an average lyric into an interesting one.

> **Why it matters:** Training yourself to push beyond the first or most obvious word that comes into your head is a great way of turning an average lyric into a good one, or a good one into a great one.

DAY 2 CHALLENGE

 10 mins

Think of <u>at least twenty words to describe color</u> that aren't any of the following:

black	**white**	**red**
blue	**green**	**yellow**
purple	**brown**	

Feel free to be as creative as you like. As well as more obvious colors that aren't on the list, you could also look for adjectives that describe other qualities but suggest color – like 'ashen' or 'luminescent'.

[DAY 3]
ONE-WORD TITLE
SEARCH

[DAY 3]

ONE-WORD TITLE SEARCH

Coming up with great titles is an essential part of the songwriting process. Sometimes it's the first thing you do. Sometimes you decide on a song's story or situation before you try and express that through a title. As long as your song ends up with a title that fits its story or situation well, it's all good.

Today you're going to try the title-first approach. You're looking for words that both grab your listeners' attention and encourage you to write something different and imaginative.

Why it matters: Choosing a great title is part of writing a great song. Sometimes all you need is that great word or phrase and everything else starts to fall together.

DAY 3 CHALLENGE

 10 mins

Come up with <u>at least twelve one-word song titles</u> that really grab people's attention or just sound compelling to you.

There are no rules about what these should or shouldn't be, but emotionally-charged words, or dramatic words, or words about some kind of pain or conflict tend to work really well – e.g. crazy, paradise, fever, fallout.

[DAY 4]
FREE WRITE #1

[DAY 4]

FREE WRITE #1

Today's challenge is the first of two free writes. If you've never tried free writing before, it's a great place to start when you're not completely sure what the lyric could be about or could be trying to say. It's a way of getting ideas and phrases down on the page that you can craft into a polished lyric later.

The challenge is really simple: write for 10 minutes without stopping. Don't filter, don't edit. Just write.

90% of what you write might be terrible – and that's fine. 95% of what you write will probably come out in free prose – without any structure, shape or rhyme – which is also fine. The goal is to get the raw material you might build your song out of on the page, without judging it or filtering yourself in any way. The goal is just to write, non-stop, and see what happens.

> **Why it matters:** Sometimes the hardest part in starting a lyric is knowing what you're trying to say. Free writing is a great way to give you the raw material of words, phrases and ideas you can craft into a lyric later.

DAY 4 CHALLENGE

 10 mins

Free Write: Pick an emotional moment in your life. Write about it in free prose for ten minutes without stopping or editing yourself.

[DAY 5]
PHRASE
BRAINSTORM

[DAY 5]

PHRASE BRAINSTORM

Saying something fresh in a lyric means avoiding anything that sounds too obvious, overused or clichéd.

At the same time, one of the keys to writing a great lyric is coming up with words or phrases that sound natural – like the things people naturally say, and the ways people express themselves in real life.

Today's challenge is about coming up with phrases that do both of those things.

> **Why it matters:** In lyric writing it's important to say things that sound both fresh and natural. Training yourself to gravitate to words and phrases that do both of these is an essential part of writing great lyrics.

DAY 5 CHALLENGE

 10 mins

Think of <u>at least ten phrases</u> that express the idea 'I love you' or 'I'm there for you'.

Have some fun with this – this challenge isn't just about looking for synonyms or rewording those two phrases. For example, 'I've got your back' and 'Call me' are both great everyday phrases that express the idea 'I'm there for you' in a more interesting way. Try finding ten more.

[DAY 6]
THE NEAR RHYME
CHALLENGE

[DAY 6]

THE NEAR RHYME CHALLENGE

The very first challenge was about finding perfect rhymes to a list of given words. Today's challenge is the same, except you're looking for near rhymes – also called half or slant rhymes.

Half rhymes are any rhymes that are not quite perfect – like 'cat' and 'sack', or 'through' and 'shoot'. You'll hear how '-at' and '-ack' are almost the same sound but not quite, and ditto '-ooh' and '-oot'. Not every song (or songwriter) uses tons of near rhymes – but plenty do because they can stop a lyric sounding too square or formal, and they open up lots of other rhyming possibilities.

The kind of rhymes you use in your songs depends mostly on personal taste and the conventions of the styles or genres you work in, but whatever you write, being able to draw on different types of rhymes is an important songwriting skill.

Why it matters: Training your brain to churn out rhyming words – including different types of rhyme – on demand is an essential songwriting skill.

DAY 6 CHALLENGE

 10 mins

Find <u>at least six near rhymes</u> for each of these words.

      [1] truth

      [2] enough

      [3] free

      [4] behind

      [5] far

Again, you can try cycling through the alphabet – 'at', 'bath', 'cart', 'date' … – but free associating to see what other, more unexpected near rhymes are out there is a great idea, since there are tons more near rhymes available than perfect rhymes.

In this case, some of the words are two-syllables – all a stress on the second syllable – so you can rhyme any one-syllable word or two-syllable word with a stress on the second syllable (e.g. 'behind' and 'round').

And as for how near the rhymes have to be? Use your own judgment. If you used 'truth' and 'cow' in a song, would anyone think you intended a rhyme? Probably not. How about 'truth' and 'cult'? Maybe. See what sounds convincing to you.

[DAY 7]
WORD FIELD #1

[DAY 7]

WORD FIELD #1

Lyrics are built out of individual words, so crafting a great lyric means being good at finding the right words to express what you're trying to say in the way you're trying to say it.

Today's challenge is about practicing that skill by connecting words with similar meaning. Then connecting those words with more words of similar meaning. Some people call this a 'word field' or a 'word web' or a 'semantic field', but what matters is the way it will help you to build a lyric out of related words.

Just like with free writing, you might not use every word you come up with to write your final lyric, but the act of putting them all down will give you more words to play around with when you do.

Why it matters: Training yourself to access your broader vocabulary and connect words with similar or related meanings will help you write lyrics faster and choose more suitable or more interesting words.

DAY 7 CHALLENGE

 10 mins

Word Field: Start with the word 'purpose' and spend ten minutes coming up with <u>related words</u> and <u>words related to those words</u>.

For example, you might start with a word like 'meaning' – which is similar to the word 'purpose' in being the thing that drives you in your life. Then you might connect the word 'meaning' with the word 'definition' – which is similar to the word 'meaning' in the sense of the literal meaning of a word or phrase.

It's up to you how you do this – some people put the starting word in the center of a blank page and connect all of the others with lines. Some people just let it come out more freeform. However you do it, just spend ten minutes coming up with as many words as you can. Aim for at least forty.

[DAY 8]
THE ACTION
CHALLENGE

[DAY 8]

THE ACTION CHALLENGE

Nice work – you're a whole week in.

Today's challenge is about the things people do. Because, if you hadn't noticed, what people say they do is not always what people actually do. And, if you haven't noticed, what people actually do is nearly always a better representation of who they actually are and what they think than the things they say.

In songwriting, you often hear this expressed as the principle 'show don't tell' – because it's always more captivating to talk about the moonlight streaming through the window than just to say the night was dark. In the same way, lyrics that talk about how she cries herself to sleep are always more evocative than lyrics that just say 'she was heartbroken'.

> **Why it matters:** Songs are about people, and people show us who they are in what they do. That's why compelling lyrics make sure to show and not just tell.

DAY 8 CHALLENGE

 10 mins

Come up with <u>at least ten things</u> a shady lover might do behind your back.

If you've ever had the luck of being with a shady significant other, you'll know first-hand they don't sit you down and say 'Hey, this isn't working'.

Instead, they *do* things that show that they're shady. They don't answer your calls. They're distant and aloof. They slide into someone else's DMs. Try and come up with at least ten other things somebody who's flaky, deceptive or just not interested might do that show you they're flaky, deceptive or just not interested.

[DAY 9]
QUICK CHORUS #1

[DAY 9]

QUICK CHORUS #1

Next up is a different kind of challenge: you're going to write a complete song section today.

I'm going to give you a lyrical hook – the word or phrase that's repeated in your chorus and encapsulates what your song is about – and ask you to build a complete chorus around it. (The lyrical hook a song uses in its chorus is usually also its title, by the way, though there are exceptions.)

Ultimately, this challenge is about filling the gaps in a lyric to build a complete chorus. But it's not just about filling those gaps with any old words – your challenge is to find words and ideas that expand on the lyrical hook idea I give you. Because that's what writing an effective chorus lyric is all about.

Why it matters: Being able to write words that focus and expand on a central idea is an essential part of creating a coherent chorus.

DAY 9 CHALLENGE

 10 mins

<u>Write an eight-line chorus.</u> **Put the lyrical hook 'If only you'd have told me' in lines 1, 3 and 7, then fill in the blank lines around this hook so the chorus works as a whole.**

The key here is coming up with words or phrases — especially in lines 2, 4 and 8 — that feel like a natural continuation or development of the lyrical hook I gave you. So line 2 could be something like 'We wouldn't be in this mess' or 'If only I'd have seen'. In lines 5 and 6 you're freer to come up with something different that's still related to the chorus's main message.

You want the chorus to sound as coherent as possible — not like the lyrical hook is being intentionally repeated three times, even if it is. It might take a few tries to come up with lines that you like, and that's fine. You can use rhymes or decide not to, but if you do, rhyming lines 2 and 4, then 6 and 8 is a great way to do it.

If only you'd have told me

…

If only you'd have told me

…

…

…

If only you'd have told me

…

[DAY 10]
WORD PAIRS
BRAINSTORM

[DAY 10]

WORD PAIRS BRAINSTORM

Today's challenge is another kind of free association challenge, but this time instead of associating similar things, you're going to be associating things that are different. Specifically, your challenge is to come up with things that are different but turn out to sound really great together.

Because, if you didn't know already, the key to creating something new is to put existing things together in a way that's never been done before. That's right – there are no completely new ideas, only new ways of combining old ideas. And that's what today's challenge is all about: creating fresh and extraordinary phrases out of existing ordinary words.

Why it matters: Part of creating something interesting and original is discovering the strange and unusual connections that are out there, just waiting to be found by anyone who's prepared to look for them.

DAY 10 CHALLENGE

 10 mins

Come up with <u>at least twelve unusual word pairs</u> that might sound interesting in a lyric.

We're talking pairs like 'electric love' or 'happy hangover' – concepts made out of two ordinary words that have maybe never been put together that way before.

If it helps, start with an ordinary word – any ordinary word – and then try other words either at random, or specific words you've chosen that seem opposite or contradictory somehow. Some of these pairs might not seem interesting to you, but that's OK. Just keep going until you find some word pairs that sound interesting.

Here are six ordinary starter words if they're helpful:

happy	average	breakup
ache	sight	Monday

[DAY 11]
FREE WRITE #2

[DAY 11]

FREE WRITE #2

So by now you've got a feel for how free writes work, and today you're going to take things to the next level.

On Day 4, you free wrote from a direct, real-life experience – because it's always important to connect the real world with the art you create. Today you're free writing about an imaginary situation – you're trying to put yourself in that situation and then let your experiences of similar situations inform what you write.

Again, the key to free writing is to write, non-stop, for ten minutes without pausing to reflect or edit yourself. Just let the words pour out without really thinking about grammar, content, style, consistency or anything like that.

Why it matters: Free writing is a great way to overcome your inner critic and just let the ideas flow. This challenge is also an opportunity to practice inventing a situation and empathizing with the person in it.

DAY 11 CHALLENGE

 10 mins

Free Write: Imagine a specific situation where you meet someone for the first time and you really like them – it could be a date, a job interview, meeting your idol, or sitting next to someone interesting on a plane. Anything. Write for ten minutes without stopping about what's going through your head.

This is a great exercise in putting yourself in someone else's shoes – like songwriters often do – and finding words that capture that situation.

It's important you pick a specific situation because that'll help guide you towards specific things to say. You could then build a lyric out of these words and phrases at a later stage.

[DAY 12]
THE LIST MAKING
CHALLENGE

[DAY 12]

THE LIST MAKING CHALLENGE

Fun fact: most lyrics are lists in one way or another: lists of ideas or thoughts or feelings or people or events or something else.

But some song lyrics use really explicit lists to build particularly tightly structured lyrics. Like Rick Astley's list of things he'll never do. Like Dua Lipa's list of new rules. Like Sebastian the crab's list of crustaceans that play wind and percussion instruments.

Sure, not every lyric will be as tightly structured as these examples, but coming up with lists of related things or ideas is an essential part of writing good lyrics.

Some of the challenges have already focused on finding lists – perfect rhymes, attention-grabbing titles, things people do. But today's is about making quick lists of specifics you might use to paint a picture or express a particular idea in a lyric.

Why it matters: At some level, most lyrics are just lists of related ideas that add up to some larger meaning or effect. So being skilled at brainstorming specific ideas is an essential part of songwriting.

DAY 12 CHALLENGE

 10 mins

Take each of these five categories and come up with <u>at least eight things</u> that belong in each.

[1] Items of clothing

[2] Restaurant chains

[3] Major world cities

[4] Car manufacturers

[5] Reasons to be happy

Coming up with forty items in ten minutes is no small feat, so try not to filter yourself and just roll with whatever comes to mind. Listing ideas in songwriting often means coming up with way more ideas than you need and then picking out the best ones, so it's OK if some of your ideas are better than others. Just aim for at least eight things in each category.

[DAY 13]
THE CONSONANCE
CHALLENGE

[DAY 13]

THE CONSONANCE CHALLENGE

Consonance is when the same or similar consonant sounds appear in quick succession in a phrase or sentence. One of the most common types of consonance is alliteration, where the consonant sounds are the beginning of words – like 'party people'. But consonance can also be looser than that – like 'happy people shopping'.

In fact, you can also create consonant effects by using letter sounds that sound similar, such as 'b' and 'p' or 'k', 'f' and 't', in quick succession – like 'frickin' tricky turtle'.

The key to writing a unified song lyric is to make its individual words feel like they belong inevitably together. The most important way to do this is through what those words mean, but you can also connect words through the way they sound – and consonance is one great way of doing that.

Why it matters: Putting consonant words nearby in a lyric is a great way to make the words sound cohesive. So training your brain to gravitate towards consonant sounds is a useful songwriting skill.

DAY 13 CHALLENGE

 10 mins

Come up with <u>at least ten consonant phrases</u> of two or more words. As usual, it's great if you can come up with phrases that make sense together and aren't just random words or syllables.

This is another challenge where you'll get better at it the more you do it, but if you're not sure where to start, pick a word to begin, focus on some of the consonant sounds in it and start brainstorming other words or phrases that feature those sounds, and just see what seems to go well together.

Here are six starting words you can use if you need them:

dance	feeling	work
guilt	ride	shop

[DAY 14]
THE BIG, BEAUTIFUL
CHALLENGE

[DAY 14]

THE BIG, BEAUTIFUL CHALLENGE

Song lyrics are a compact form: you don't have a ton of space to say what you have to say. In a three- or four-minute song you have maybe 300 words to play with, and plenty of those words will be repeated several times throughout your song – like its chorus.

So when it comes to writing lyrics, being able to choose your words with laser precision is an important skill. You want to choose the right words – the ones that will have the most impact and say exactly what you're trying to say.

In practice, that can mean coming up with a more obvious or trite way of saying something, and then searching just a bit harder to find a less obvious word that does an even better job of capturing what you want to say.

That's what today's challenge is all about.

> **Why it matters:** Simple, everyday words usually work great in song lyrics. But sometimes there's a less obvious word that really captures your song's message.

DAY 14 CHALLENGE

 10 mins

Come up with <u>at least fifteen words</u> that mean 'beautiful'.

You could start with words that are just straight-up synonyms, like 'stunning', but you can also look for words that could mean beautiful but that aren't exact synonyms – like 'radiant'. If you find fifteen before the ten minutes is up, keep going.

[DAY 15]
THE SIMPLICITY
CHALLENGE

[DAY 15]

THE SIMPLICITY CHALLENGE

One of the fundamental skills of great writing – in any format – is being able to say things as simply as possible. Unless you have a good reason not to, it's better to say 'because' instead of 'for the reason that' because 'because' is simpler. It packs more punch.

This is especially true in lyric writing because – as we talked about in the last challenge – lyrics are already such a compact form.

But the truth is, most people aren't great at simplicity because it takes practice. It takes practice to use the fewest words that make the biggest impact. It takes practice to see which words add meaning, style or context and which are just dead weight you can cut or swap for a different word that does add something.

Today's challenge is an opportunity to practice this essential skill.

Why it matters: In a lyric, you want to say things as compactly as possible.

DAY 15 CHALLENGE

 10 mins

Take each of these wordy phrases and find a simpler way to say them.

[1] The day after today we'll go shopping.

[2] There are all kinds of reasons why.

[3] It's a situation that's a strange one.

[4] At the time of my arrival I knew it was too late.

[5] Yeah, I guess I could sort of maybe do that.

[6] The girl with the red hat on her head.

[7] Nothing in the world is more important than sleeping.

[8] My love for you is completely, 100% unconditional.

[9] She went and did a terrible thing.

[10] I headed out at the usual time of 8 in the morning.

Sometimes there's a single word that can say the same thing as a handful of them. Sometimes there are words you can cut and no meaning or style is really lost. Sometimes, of course, this is more opinion than fact – so you have to figure out what you think.

So don't panic if you can't shorten each line by more than a word or two, but there are definitely snappier ways to say each of them.

[DAY 16]
LONGER TITLE
SEARCH

[DAY 16]

LONGER TITLE SEARCH

All right, you're halfway there. So let's celebrate the halfway point with another song title challenge — though this time you're searching for titles of three or more words.

As we talked about on Day 3, you want a song's title to match closely with its idea, story or situation. Today is an opportunity to find longer phrases or sentences that sound intriguing, provocative or capture an interesting idea somehow.

Why it matters: A great title is a great way into a new song. And a title can be anything from a single word to a complete sentence in length.

DAY 16 CHALLENGE

 10 mins

Come up with <u>at least ten interesting song titles</u> of three words or more.

There are basically two ways to tackle this, now you have more words to play with.

One, like we saw before, is to come up with words or phrases that are dramatic, interesting or emotionally charged somehow – like 'My Tired Heart' or 'Out in the Cold' or 'Something to Keep Me Strong'.

The other is to try and come up with interesting or fresh phrases that express something ordinary in a way we've never heard before. I'm thinking about phrases like 'Locked Out of Heaven' or 'Total Eclipse of the Heart'.

And again, just see what sparks you. There's no right and wrong. If the title phrases sound interesting to you, then they're great solutions.

[DAY 17]
CONVERSATIONAL
PHRASES

[DAY 17]

CONVERSATIONAL PHRASES

One of the cornerstones of good songwriting is writing lyrics that sound conversational, because a song lyric is sung by someone to someone else.

This is one of the reasons that writing song lyrics is hard – carefully constructing a lyric while also making it sound like someone just came up with it is tough. And like always, it's something that you get better at with practice.

But whatever level you're at, sometimes you express something awkwardly on your first try and then have to reword it to express it in a more natural way. (As we'll talk about in the final challenge, "Great songs aren't written, they're rewritten.")

And that's exactly what you're going to practice in today's challenge.

Why it matters: Great song lyrics don't sound like they were carefully crafted – they sound like an ordinary person saying them on the spot. Training yourself to write conversationally is an essential lyric writing skill.

DAY 17 CHALLENGE

 10 mins

Rewrite these awkward-sounding lyrics to make them more conversational.

[1] I do not think I can come.

[2] In my opinion the party was really great.

[3] He drove away in his new vehicle.

[4] The way he treated her was frightful.

[5] On some occasions things went particularly well.

[6] The sex was average, I think.

[7] What can a person do?

[8] It was a particularly stylish way to spend a weekend.

That might be as simple as turning 'is not' into 'isn't' or 'ain't', or it might involve more substantial rewriting – like changing a formal word like 'car' to more of a slang word like 'ride' or rephrasing the entire sentence. Again, you'll have to use your judgment: if it's the sort of thing you'd hear someone say naturally in conversation, it works.

You can also think about adding informal words like 'yeah' or 'um' to these phrases if you think that helps them sound conversational.

[DAY 18]
PLAYING WITH
METER

[DAY 18]

PLAYING WITH METER

Meter in songwriting – and poetry – is about where the stress patterns fall in words. Stresses are the extra weight you get on some syllables, like LOOK-ing and Bei-JING. (Which is why I said on Day 1 that those words don't really rhyme.)

Generally speaking, songwriters don't have to worry about meter in too much detail in the way poets might. But it's still important to have a solid grasp of how meter works, because often rewriting a word or phrase of a lyric means replacing what you've already got with something that matches the original stress pattern.

So today you're going to practice playing around with meter, and writing to a predetermined stress pattern.

Why it matters: Virtually nobody is writing songs today to a regular meter or stress pattern, but as songwriters it's still important to be quick in identifying how words are stressed so you can write effectively.

DAY 18 CHALLENGE

 10 mins

Write <u>five lyric lines with this regular stress pattern</u> (u for unstressed, S for stressed):

u – S – u – S – u – S – u – S

If you're interested, this pattern is known as iambic quadrameter (made up of four iambs, a unit made up of an unstressed then stressed syllable). A well-known example is 'I WAN-dered LONE-ly AS a CLOUD'.

As always, the goal of these lines is not just to come up with any old words that fit the pattern, but to write something that has some kind of meaning. If in doubt, sketch out what you mean first, *then* try to find a way to say it that fits the stress pattern.

If it helps, here are five two-syllable phrases to get you started:

[1] Sometimes…

[2] I wish…

[3] But still…

[4] Again…

[5] You said…

[DAY 19]
WORD FIELD #2

[DAY 19]

WORD FIELD #2

Today you've got another word field challenge. It's the same deal as on Day 7, only with a new word.

It's another chance to build a word field that you could then use to write a fully-fledged lyric.

> **Why it matters:** In a nutshell, writing lyrics is about finding the right words for each song, and practicing coming up with related or connected words is a great way to develop or explore a new song idea.

DAY 19 CHALLENGE

 10 mins

Word Field: Start with the word 'pain' and spend ten minutes coming up with <u>related words</u> and <u>words related to those words</u>.

Exactly like before, start with 'pain' and find some related words – like 'anguish' – then see where those words lead – like 'longing'. You can draw a web and connect the related words or you can just write freestyle on the page.

Just make sure you spend the full ten minutes coming up with words and again, aim for at least forty.

[DAY 20]
THE SH*T YOU LOVE
CHALLENGE

[DAY 20]

THE SH*T YOU LOVE CHALLENGE

Great work. You're into the twenties and powering ahead.

Today's challenge ties together a handful of skills you've already practiced: it's another type of list challenge, it's another challenge about specifics, and it's another challenge that is a chance to practice the 'show don't tell' principle.

It's the kind of thing you'd do as a songwriter once you've figured out your song's big idea, then start building words, phrases and ideas you could craft into a finished lyric.

Why it matters: One way to help build an effective lyric is to sketch out ideas around a specific theme or purpose that you can then use in a complete lyric.

DAY 20 CHALLENGE

 10 mins

Think of someone you love or admire – it could be a love interest, or someone else – and come up with <u>at least fifteen specific things you love or admire about them.</u>

These things could be really superficial – like their eyes or that they're tall – but it's also a good idea to find more meaningful characteristics or behaviors – like how they smile a lot, or how they know your go-to coffee is an Americano, two sugars.

As usual, the goal is to be specific: you're trying to come up with ideas you could use in a song lyric to paint a really clear picture of who that person is and why they're special to you.

[DAY 21]
CONTEMPORARY
RHYMES SEARCH

[DAY 21]

CONTEMPORARY RHYMES SEARCH

On Day 17 we looked at ways to make a lyric sound more conversational. Another way to do this is to use words and phrases you probably wouldn't find in *The Oxford English Dictionary* but you would at urbandictionary.com.

Using slang is also a great way to freshen up the rhymes you use – like 'dope' and 'hope', or 'viral' and 'spiral'. That's because the less time a word has been around, the less chance it's going to end up sounding clichéd as part of a rhyming pair.

Today you're going to practice using both of these ideas at once: finding some contemporary slang words and some great rhymes to go with them.

Why it matters: Using contemporary words and phrases is a great way of keeping a lyric sounding fresh and conversational.

DAY 21 CHALLENGE

 10 mins

Come up with <u>at least twelve contemporary or slang words and find rhymes for them</u>.

A great place to start with this is to think about words or concepts you maybe wouldn't find in a dictionary but you either hear in real life, on TV, on Twitter etc. Or just think of words that sound particularly fresh or that particularly represent right now.

Then try coming up with good rhymes for those words: either just one extra word to make a pair, or a list of rhymes if they come to you.

It's up to you whether you want to stick to perfect rhymes or use near rhymes as well. And finally, you don't need to rhyme slang words with other slang words, though if you find any pairs like that you get bonus points.

[DAY 22]
SONG IDEA SEARCH

[DAY 22]

SONG IDEA SEARCH

We've been circling round this challenge already in the song title challenges, but today you're going to practice fleshing out an initial idea for a song more completely.

A great song idea is about answering three important questions: who is singing, who they're singing to, and what they're trying to say. (Plus, it often helps to put these three parts into perspective by trying to figure out *why* the singer wants to say what they're saying.)

In short, answering these three (or four) questions is about coming up with strong situations, where all of those answers make sense together as a unit.

And as we'll explore in more detail on Day 28, whether those situations are fictional or truthful doesn't matter. What matters is that you come up with situations that *could* exist in real life – that seem real even if they're invented.

> **Why it matters:** Whatever part of a song comes first, a song works best when it focuses on a single idea or situation.

DAY 22 CHALLENGE

 10 mins

Come up with <u>at least three fleshed-out song ideas</u>. This means answering three fundamental questions:

- **Who is singing?**

- **Who are they singing to?**

- **What are they trying to say?**

For simplicity, it's a good idea to choose one of two very effective formats – a song that is sung by one person to one other person (like a love song), or a song that is sung by an artist to the world.

Once you've decided which, try to define what your singer's main message – or thesis – could be, given the choices you've made so far. (You could even use some of the ideas you came up with in previous challenges – like a title or phrase – to help you do this.)

The key is to come up with something that feels like coherent song idea – a situation or concept where your answers to the three fundamental questions above make sense as a unit.

Plus, if you get three ideas together well before ten minutes is up, start thinking about why your singer might be saying what they're saying. Try and come up with some backstory that puts their situation into perspective.

[DAY 23]
THE ASSONANCE CHALLENGE

[DAY 23]

THE ASSONANCE CHALLENGE

We've already looked at consonance – repeating the same consonant sound in nearby words – and today's challenge is about assonance – repeating the same vowel sound in nearby words.

You find assonance in phrases like 'oh so cold' or 'the freakin' weekend' where the 'oh' or 'ee' sound happens a few times in quick succession. I'm sure you'll agree these phrases sound way more compelling than 'very cold' or 'the crazy weekend'.

In these examples, 'oh' and 'so' are perfect rhymes, and most people would call 'freakin'' and 'weekend' near rhymes. But while assonance includes rhyme, it also includes more loosely connected words like 'behold' and 'sofa' and 'adonis', all with an 'oh' sound.

While rhyme is a tool that's mostly used at the ends of lines, peppering your lyric with assonant words where you can is a great way to give your audience a tiny endorphin boost as they pass by.

Why it matters: Assonance is a great tool to make any set of words more compelling and more interesting to listen to. As a lyricist, it's good to train your brain to gravitate towards assonant words in what you write.

DAY 23 CHALLENGE

 10 mins

Come up with <u>at least eight assonant phrases</u>. These could be anything from two or three words to short sentences. The key is to come up with words that repeat the same vowel sounds enough times that it sounds really compelling to listen to.

If you're not sure where to start, first pick a word or phrase that seems like a good topic idea – like 'city', 'longing', or 'party'. Then pick the word's most dominant vowel sound – the short 'i' in 'city', the short 'o' in 'longing', or the longer 'ah' in 'party' – and try to come up with tons of other words that feature those sounds.

Then see whether there's any meaning you can string out of all the words you've collected. Like always, the best phrases are going to mean something or capture something, not just be assonant nonsense phrases.

So you might end up with something like 'hip little city', or if you wanted something longer, 'this hip little city which we live in'.

[DAY 24]
THE VULNERABILITY
CHALLENGE

[DAY 24]

THE VULNERABILITY CHALLENGE

Songwriting is about revelation and vulnerability – it's about revealing the inner world of whoever's singing. And because music affects us on a deep, instinctual level, songwriting is a really great medium to express this kind of vulnerability or candidness in a deep and profound way.

That means part of your job in writing lyrics is being comfortable going for those deep and sometimes uncomfortable emotions – whether you're writing songs for yourself, or just connecting with your own emotional experiences to write for someone else.

Getting comfortable with being vulnerable about your own feelings is the key to writing great lyrics that connect deeply with other people. And today's challenge is an opportunity to push yourself into those vulnerable places that might be beyond your usual comfort zone.

Why it matters: Big and profound emotions are key in a lot of great song lyrics. But as writers we can only go there if we're prepared to connect with our own big and profound emotions.

DAY 24 CHALLENGE

 10 mins

Think of something important you wish you'd said to someone but didn't, or you wish you could say to someone but can't. For ten minutes, write down exactly what you'd say to them, in prose. Be as honest and vulnerable as you can.

Seriously: push yourself to say what you have to say as truthfully as you can. Don't filter yourself – but this time, if you realize you could make what you've written more open and honest, you're welcome to edit or rewrite some of it if it means you go deeper.

This isn't just another free write – it's a chance to delve into your own life and get comfortable expressing feelings that might feel raw and uncomfortable to you.

You don't have to share what you write with anyone – so there's no reason to hold back. Your goal is to push yourself to the limit of how open and vulnerable you're able to be in what you write.

[DAY 25]
THE OPENING LINE
CHALLENGE

[DAY 25]

THE OPENING LINE CHALLENGE

If you write a newspaper headline or blog post title, your goal is to grab people's attention. Likewise, the very first line of a song is a great place to grab people's attention to make sure they stick around for the rest of it.

Some great first lines are questions: "Do you ever feel like a plastic bag? ..."

Some are dramatic images: "I was so high, I did not recognize the fire burning in her eyes ..." (Which, for the record, is also a great assonant phrase.)

And some are provocative, intriguing or attention-grabbing in some other way: "It might sound crazy, what I'm 'bout to say ...".

Whatever techniques you decide to use, there's an art to writing attention-grabbing first lines, and that's what today's challenge is about.

> **Why it matters:** In lyric writing, it's important to be able to come up with lines that grab your listener's attention right from the start.

DAY 25 CHALLENGE

 10 mins

Come up with <u>at least eight attention-grabbing opening lines</u> that could begin a song's first verse.

It's up to you how you do this, but here are four great tactics:

1) Write a line that's dramatic or intriguing.

2) Write a line that asks a direct question.

3) Write a line that makes a provocative statement.

4) Write a line that describes a bold image.

[DAY 26]
QUICK VERSE

[DAY 26]

QUICK VERSE

Today's challenge is an opportunity to write a complete first verse from an opening line I'll give you.

As you practiced on Day 9 – and you'll do again on Day 29 – the job of a chorus lyric is to get right to the heart of what your song is about in a really direct way.

Your verse lyrics, on the other hand, are where you set the scene for what the song is about and start giving us the details that tell your song's story.

So the key to this challenge is to do exactly that: to decide on a specific situation or idea, and start telling us about it in the eight-line verse you're going to write.

> **Why it matters:** Your first verse is the place you start bringing your listener into the world and story of your song. So being able to build a verse out of a ton of specific ideas is an important songwriting skill.

DAY 26 CHALLENGE

 10 mins

<u>**Write a first draft of an eight-line verse**</u> **given this first line:**

    It's been a long, long time comin',

    ...

If you feel confident enough to dive in, you can go right ahead. But if you need any pointers, here are three quick tips:

1)   Like you did on Day 22, your first job is to decide who is singing, who they are singing to, and what the song is about. You probably want to either write a third-person song that tells a story to everyone else, or a first-person song that has a message to a specific person.

2)   Once you've answered these three questions, think about what specifically could have 'been a long time coming'. What is the main message of your song?

3)   From there, brainstorm other specific ideas that are relevant to the situation, or that help explain or set up that situation. From there you can craft those ideas into a lyric.

It's up to you how you play around with structure and rhyme, but I recommend you keep each line short and focused – no more than 12 words. To keep things simple, I recommend you finish lines 2 and 4, then 6 and 8 with rhyming pairs, like you did on Day 9.

[DAY 27]
DE-TONGUE
TWISTER
CHALLENGE

[DAY 27]

DE-TONGUE TWISTER CHALLENGE

Tongue twisters are fun to say but not fun to sing. So when writing lyrics you want to pay attention to all of the consonant sounds you're using and keep an eye out for any places you end up packing too many different consonant sounds close together.

The acid test for this is to speak your lyric out loud so you can get a feel for spots that are awkward to say – because if they're awkward to say, they'll probably be awkward to sing too.

Generally speaking, you want to avoid using tons of consonant-heavy words – like 'growth' or 'stretch' – and gravitate as much as possible to words with one or no consonant sounds at either end – like 'too' or 'are'. Naturally, you can't always do that, but training yourself to pick out more easily-singable words when you can is an essential songwriting skill.

Today's challenge is about putting that skill into practice.

Why it matters: For a lyric to have the most impact, it's important it's easy enough to sing. That means looking out for places your lyric packs too many consonants close together and rewriting any really tricky phrases.

DAY 27 CHALLENGE

 10 mins

Take each of these eight phrases and try to express the same idea in a way that's easier to sing.

> [1] Red lorries are the best.
>
> [2] I felt like sticking stickers to all four walls.
>
> [3] I'm growing gradually into something different.
>
> [4] Strewth guys, it's so bright outside.
>
> [5] Peter Piper got three different Grammys.
>
> [6] People can't change the things they want to.
>
> [7] Spring wasn't giving us what we needed.
>
> [8] Tricky days might be real challenging but they're necessary.

Expressing the same idea might mean mixing up the exact meaning but creating the same kind of effect – so 'lorry' could become 'van', and you could express the idea of 'the best' with the word 'love' instead. You can even reword or reorganize a phrase completely if you want.

And like with a couple of the other challenges, it's up to you to decide what you think is worth improving or not. So even if you just take out one spot where the consonants are backing up, that's great.

[DAY 28]
THE UNIVERSAL
TRUTH CHALLENGE

[DAY 28]

THE UNIVERSAL TRUTH CHALLENGE

Songs don't have to be based on true real life events to affect us. Lots of songs, novels and movies are completely fictional, but they move us because we see our own lives in the people they're about.

These universal truths or universal experiences are powerful sources for great song ideas because the more universal a song idea is, the more people it's likely to resonate with, and the more deeply it's likely to resonate with them.

In previous challenges you've come up with specific song ideas or titles, but in this challenge we're less worried about the specifics and more about the universal truths behind a new song idea.

> **Why it matters:** Lots of great songs are based on common experiences and universal truths, so as songwriters it's important to be able to identify these.

DAY 28 CHALLENGE

 10 mins

Think of <u>at least eight universal truths or experiences</u> that could be the basis for a great song.

For example, falling in love is a common song idea because it's such a universal experience – virtually everyone can relate. But try and find some more – come up with eight more types of situations and/or experiences most people can associate with.

If it helps, think about the most emotional or affecting moments in your life, or the lives of people you know. Then ask yourself what about those moments was universal.

Your universal truths don't have to have literally happened to everyone, ever – but try to go as deep as possible to find emotionally significant experiences that most people have experienced – or will experience – at some point in their lives.

[DAY 29]
QUICK CHORUS #2

[DAY 29]

QUICK CHORUS #2

Today's challenge is another chance to write an eight-line chorus to a given lyrical hook.

You'll get more freedom to structure the chorus in whatever way you like this time, but the goal is the same as on Day 9: you're trying to fill in the blanks with words and phrases that complement your lyrical hook and expand on it with other ideas and images.

> **Why it matters:** Writing an effective chorus is about writing words that explore and grow from a single idea.

DAY 29 CHALLENGE

 10 mins

Write an eight-line chorus. Use the lyrical hook 'flicker' at least twice. It's up to you how you repeat it – but if you want a plan, try including it somewhere in at least lines 1 and 5. Then complete the other lines so the chorus works as a whole.

First, you probably want to decide how you'd like to use the word 'flicker' – at the start of the phrase, like 'Flicker, I can't help looking at you ...', at the end or in the middle of the phrase, like 'You make my heart flicker ...', or just as an attention-grabbing one-word line.

Then, like before, try to build a fuller lyric around the word or phrase you just completed by adding other words and phrases that grow naturally out of what you've already got. You can use the skills you practiced in other challenges – like coming up with a list of words related to the word 'flicker', or listing a ton of reasons someone might make someone or something flicker.

Flicker ...

...

...

...

Flicker ...

...

...

...

[DAY 30]
VERSE REWRITE

[DAY 30]

VERSE REWRITE

Alrighty. It's the last challenge – and I picked a fun one.

Today's challenge is a rewriting challenge. If you've been writing a while you'll know that rewriting is one of the most important but most difficult parts of turning an OK lyric into a great one.

And while rewriting is generally one of the worst things songwriters have to do, there is one simple way to make it one of the best things songwriters get to do: rewrite someone else's work.

So that's what you're going to do today. You get to tinker away at fixing my bad first draft – which means with every improvement you make you get to tell yourself you must be way smarter than me.

But seriously – being able to rewrite and refine what you write (or someone else writes) is one of the most important skills songwriters have to learn. It's the only way to create your best work.

So settle in. Tinker away. See how much you can improve what's on the page.

> **Why it matters:** Great songs aren't written, they're rewritten. Being able to turn an OK draft into a great one is an essential songwriting skill.

DAY 30 CHALLENGE

 10 mins

Spend ten minutes improving this OK first draft:

> Riding down the highway
>
> And the wind is blowing through our hair.
>
> We are running [from it all…?]
>
> But if truth be told we just don't care.
>
> As every mile [passes / goes ?] by
>
> Everything we pass seems to speed along.
>
> But that look in [his / her] eyes keeps me going,
>
> So I've gotta find the courage to say what's going on …

You've done some specific rewriting challenges already, but this challenge is freer: just use what you know about lyric writing to improve my OK first draft, including the spots I left unfinished.

You could make some of the ideas more specific or imaginative, you could make some of the language more interesting, you could make some of the wording snappier or more singable, or you could just tweak places that sound awkward or un-conversational to you.

Don't be afraid to rework some of the lines or phrases completely or even rewrite whole chunks to express the same idea in a better way. As always, use your own judgment: your only goal is to end up with something you think is better than my first draft.

TAKE A BOW – NOW WHAT'S NEXT?

TAKE A BOW – NOW WHAT'S NEXT?

Congratulations! That's all thirty challenges done. Whether they were a walk in the park or a serious uphill climb, sticking out all thirty on a set schedule is no small feat. So bravo. Take a bow.

So what happens now?

Well, that's your call.

One thing you can do is jump right into writing whatever you want to write, while focusing on applying the skills you honed in the challenges. So write what you like, but try working a bit harder when searching for a more interesting word, writing lines that sound effortless and conversational, or pushing your lyrics into a more emotionally vulnerable place.

Another great thing you can do is to start turning some of your sketches and ideas from the challenges into full songs. You could take some of the title ideas you came up with, or the free writes you did, or the lists you created and use that material to inspire complete songs.

If you're looking for more challenges, you'll probably also enjoy my *30-Day Creativity Challenge* – designed to do exactly what you just did for your lyric-writing brain for your creative brain. Like this book, they're thirty daily ten-minute challenges, only they'll make you smarter, faster and bolder at creating *anything* new.

(You might also want to keep this book on hand somewhere – redoing a handful of the challenges is a great way to motivate yourself if you're feeling blocked sometime. You could even take the whole challenge again in six months' or a year's time – though the challenges will be the same, you won't, so you'll probably come up with totally different solutions.)

And as you might know, if you're looking specifically for new songwriting ideas and inspiration there's plenty of free content you can access at thesongfoundry.com.

Other than that, your biggest challenge now is to keep going. To keep writing, to keep trying new things and to keep growing as an artist. And whatever that looks like, with these thirty challenges under your belt I hope they're the most exciting songs you've written yet.

Happy writing, compadre. Go knock 'em dead.

ALSO BY ED BELL: *THE ART OF SONGWRITING*

The Art of Songwriting is a unique songwriting guide that's not about learning rules and following methods, but about **how to think, create and live like a songwriter**.

It covers all the big concepts that go into making great songs – not just the craft of songwriting, but how creativity works and what it means to be an artist.

The Art of Songwriting is available as an eBook at **thesongfoundry.com/ebook** and in paperback online and in bookstores.

For more tools, ideas and inspiration,

visit **thesongfoundry.com**